Community Projects

 CHILDRENS PRESS, CHICAGO

Art Director
Thomas Petiet, M.F.A.

Senior Editors
Edith Wolter, B.S.
Susan Keezer

Contributors
Mary Rush, M.F.A.
Nancy Muhlbach, M.A.
Sharon Irvine, B.A.
Jerry Gillmore, B.A.
Mary White, B.A.
Virginia Foster, A.B.

Readability Consultants
Donald E.P. Smith, Ph.D.
School of Education
University of Michigan

Judith K. Smith, Ph.D.
University of Michigan

Instructional Development Consultant
Joel B. Fleming, M.A.
Instructional Development & Technolog
Michigan State University

Synectics Consultant
Gershom Clark Morningstar, M.A.
President, Wolverine-Morningstar Media

Library Consultant
Noel Winkler, M.A.L.S.
Lecturer, Children's Literature
Elementary Librarian, Media Center
School of Education
University of Michigan

Contents

Look around you. Do you see anything that you could do to make your neighborhood prettier . . . your family or neighbors happier? How about organizing a clean-up crew to rake leaves or plant a garden in a vacant lot? Why not set up a babysitting service on election day or a school-based tutoring agency? Plan a parade to celebrate a national holiday, have a rummage sale, or start a drive to collect toys and other goods for the needy.

There are many things you and your friends can do to make your world a better place to live. Do some investigating on your own. Compare prices, check values, see exactly what you are getting for your money. Write letters to government officials supporting or opposing new legislation.

This book is packed with ideas that will benefit you, your friends, and your community. But no matter what project you select there are a few things you must do.

- You must be organized.
- Plan your goal and figure out what you must to do to get there.
- Make rules for your group and follow them. Have committees if the group is large.
- Hold meetings to check on your progress and to solve any problems that might come up.

Most of the projects mentioned in this book you can do by yourself. But if you need help, ask for it. An older brother or sister, a parent, or your teachers would be happy to help a group that works for the good of the community. Being involved in the world around you and doing something for someone else is exciting and very rewarding. Try it and see.

Community Caretakers

Spring Clean the Fall Mess

Last Fall's leftovers always show up when the snow melts.

CALL a dozen or more kids together to organize a clean-up day. For practice, pick up scraps of paper, twigs and a wandering can or two from your own yard.

ARM each cleaner with a big trash bag and a brown bag lunch.

MARCH to the nearest park. Divide into teams of two. Each team can clean up one area in the park. Fill those trash bags!

WORK for a couple of hours or until lunchtime, whichever comes first. Take a lunch break. After lunch, have a game of softball. Finish tidying up the park.

TIE the tops of the trash bags and put them in waste cans. Or each kid could take one home for the trash collector.

6

TURN IN any valuable things you find to the police or park rangers.

OFFER to clean up the playgrounds at school the same way. Take time to swing after cleaning.

GET the group together to do roadside clean-up. Bring a wagon along to tote pop bottles and cans.

SPOT CHECK the areas you clean every couple of weeks. More trash? Bag it.

CHECK the newspaper. See if any of the trash you collect can be sold. The jingling of coins in your jeans is quite pleasant.

7

Baby Corral

ORGANIZE a baby-sitting service at the polls for the voters' youngsters.

CHECK the newspaper to find out when and where elections will be held.

GET your friends to help you collect some safe toys. Scrub the toys after each election.

MAKE a foldable fence out of boxes to take to the polls. Take the tops and bottoms off seven large cardboard boxes. Cut open one corner of each box. Spread the boxes out flat. Tape them together end to end with masking tape. Paint some neat pictures on both sides of the fence. Fold the fence along the taped seams. Tie it with twine to keep it from springing open.

HUSTLE the fence, toys, and sitters to the voting place. Go as early as you can on election day. Set up the fence near a wall. Station one sitter near the door. He directs voters to the corral.

MAKE name tags for all sitters. Wear them.

MAKE two sets of name tags for each child. Use colored paper and masking tape. Make a circle of tape with the sticky side out. Press the circle against the back of the tag after the name has been printed on it. Pat the tag on the back of the child so he can't reach it. Put the other tag on parent. If new sitters are in the corral when the parent returns, tags can be matched so the right baby goes with the right parent.

PACK UP the toys and fence when it's over. Clean up any spills.

You have helped others to exercise a special right.

Who won the election?

9

Vacant Lot? Green Spot!

TURN a weedy, dull piece of ground into a green spot. Make a place for sitting down and dreaming.

STROLL around your neighborhood with some other kids. Make a list of areas that could use some beauty treatment.

ASK the neighbors near the areas you want to work on who the owners are. Contact each owner. Offer to clean up his lot. Weed it and brighten it with some flowers.

FIX UP the extensions, if you can't find a vacant lot. Those are the spaces of earth between sidewalk and curb. They are often bald.

SET UP work teams. Everybody helps with the first clean up. Gather trash, bag it, and throw it away. Divide weeding, raking, seeding, and planting among the teams.

STUDY a simple gardening book. It will help you decide what flowers you can plant in your space.

FENCE OFF the freshly seeded areas with string and sticks. Then people won't walk on them. You can't do much about the birds.

FIND an old bench. Paint it a bright color and place it in the green spot. Also add a waste can. Put some bricks in the bottom of it so the wind won't carry it off.

ASSIGN each team a turn at keeping the area nice. Every week or two a team should clean up the spot, get rid of junk and do some weeding. Don't forget to water the flowers.

POST a sign inviting walkers to rest on the bench or grass.

If you have lots of flowers, take some bouquets to people who need cheering up.

Bloomers & Roomers

FIND an open area near your school or in your neighborhood to use for nature study.

GET some kids together to plan how to develop the space.

GO to the library. Check out books on plants, flowers, trees, and birds.

STUDY the area's trees and plants. Find out their names by checking the books.

MAKE identification signs for all the plants, trees, and flowers. Use permanent ink. Place the signs in front of the growing things.

HAUL in some rocks or bricks. Use them to mark walking paths through the area.

INVITE some birds to live in the nature area. Build a birdhouse and feeding station. Save bread scraps. These can be the salad of the bird cafe.

SUPPLY a waste can at the entrance of the area to capture litter.

SET UP a schedule of nature watchers. They must visit the area regularly. They can keep a log of which birds are visiting and what flowers are blooming.

LEAVE some big rocks in the space for the sunbathing snakes.

Grades Up Agency

FORM a tutoring service with some other kids. Get kids who are good readers or know their math.

DESIGN a form with blank spaces for the client's name, grade, and telephone number. List the subjects your group will tutor. Ask the client to check the subjects he is interested in.

MAKE UP lots of forms to pass out at school. Place a collection box in a handy place for form deposit.

EMPTY the box daily.

SET UP a calendar showing which subjects will be tutored on which days. Math on Mondays? Reading on Wednesdays? Recess on Saturdays?

MATCH clients with tutors. Write the clients' name on the calendar in the right square. Call each client to tell him his appointment date and time.

GIVE each client the name of his tutor and where they will meet. It might well be on the south bench in the park.

Some clients might need just a couple of appointments. Others might come for several weeks.

FIND OUT from the clients if your service is really helping. Listen to the clients' comments. They will have good suggestions.

PLAN a once-a-month biking tour, hike, or picnic for clients and tutors.

USE the skills you are teaching to figure out how far you will hike. Figure how many hot dogs you need. Plan good routing for the bicycles.

A BASIC PARADE

GET the kids in your neighborhood to plan a parade. Lemonade and cookies will help you plan.

CHOOSE a theme for the parade. It might be a special holiday parade. How about a "School's out—Yippee" parade?

MAKE floats using wagons.

TIE a flat piece of cardboard to the bed of a wagon. Shape chicken wire into the form you need for the flat. Staple the wire to the cardboard on the wagon. Stuff the holes in the wire with colored facial tissue to make a design.

The kids who don't make floats can ride their bikes or tricycles in the parade. They can weave crepe paper streamers through the spokes of their wheels. Bells on the handle bars will make a happy sound. Tie on some balloons.

FIND about 12 kids for the parade band. They can play rhythm instruments and whistles. Add a drum and some horns. The band can do some dance steps while parading.

CHOOSE a parade marshal to get everyone lined up. Let the band be first.

When the marshal gives a signal, the parade starts. The band plays fast and loud marching music. Don't have a cramped parade. Leave about six feet of space between each float or bike.

GIVE an award for the best float. The fanciest bicycle deserves a prize too.

TAKE the parade to a shady spot for a brown bag lunch. After a rest, take the parade back along the same route. Pick up any litter the gang left.

That was nice.

Age to Age

MAKE a list of all the elderly people in your neighborhood.

GET your pals together to offer help to the older neighbors.

VISIT each person on your list. Find out what you can do to help him or her. Here are some things you and your friends can do:

> write letters and mail them
> shop for groceries
> clean screens and storm
>   windows
> fix lunch once a week
> mow lawns
> sweep porches and sidewalks
> rake leaves
> carry out trash
> shovel snow
> visit just to chat once a week
> telephone daily to see if
>   person is okay
> make holiday visits.

Can you think of other things?

PUT the names of each older person on index cards. List the help they need on the cards.

ELECT a secretary to keep track of the helpers and who they are helping. The secretary can match the kids to the jobs they like best.

DECIDE which days your group can do all these good deeds. Let the people know when you will be visiting. Don't forget to go. If you can't keep the date, call the person and set up a new date.

KEEP IN TOUCH with these people on holidays. Make and deliver birthday treats.

Love.

19

Toy Round-Up

ASK your friends and their friends to sort out toys they no longer need. Ask them for books, games, and puzzles. Make sure everything is in good shape. Puzzles must have all their pieces. No missing pages from books, please.

GET all the goods together. Plan a work day to fix up all the toys. Some might need repainting or a couple of screws. If puzzle boxes are in sad shape, cover them with bright paper. A touch of toothpaste will take spots off book covers.

MAKE a list of all the things your gang has fixed up. Divide the list by "baby toys," "toddler toys," and so on.

LOOK UP day care centers or nurseries in the yellow pages of the telephone book. Write down a few of them and their telephone numbers.

CALL each center on your list. Tell the person who answers your name. Explain that you and your friends have some spruced up toys you would like to give away. Read the list of toys and ask if the center can use any of them.

DELIVER the toys the nurseries or centers can use.

Toys are never outgrown—someone always needs them.

Getting Around

PUBLIC·LIBRARY	Yes	No
Feature	✓	
Ramps	✓	
Elevators		✓
Low Phones	✓	
Doorways	✓	
Aisles		✓
Braille		✓
Seeing Eye Dogs		

MAKE an inspection tour of public buildings in your city or town.

ASSIGN the library to a couple of kids, city hall to another pair. Give grocery stores to others, and churches to another team. What other buildings do lots of people visit? Theatres, restaurants, museums? Sure. Cover as many buildings as you can.

TAKE pads of paper and pencils with you. Write down each building's name as you visit. Find out which buildings are the easiest for people in wheelchairs to get into and move in. There should be ramps for wheelchairs and wide doorways. How wide are the aisles? Look to see if there are pay telephones placed low on the walls.

While you are at it, do some inspecting for the blind. Check for Braille markings on elevators. Find out how seeing eye dogs are handled in each building.

TAKE notes, writing down under each building's name what you found.

On the street, check curbs at cross walks. See if a wheelchair can go up and down easily. Jot down the good places. Is there a button on the traffic signal post to stop traffic for pedestrians? Could it be reached by a wheelchair passenger?

CHECK parking lots. Are there special spaces marked for handicapped drivers?

GET all the information together to make one big list. Ask someone to type it. Make lots of copies on a duplicating machine.

PUT giveaway copies of your list in waiting rooms at the doctors' offices and hospitals. Others could be put in the library. Think of other places.

DELIVER lists to handicapped people you know.

CORNER OF MAIN AND THIRD STREET		
Feature	Yes	No
Low Curbs		
Traffic Button		✔
		✔
Must go to bank drive to get to street.		

Signs of the Times

ORGANIZE a sign shop. Get a bunch of kids together who like to make signs.

DESIGN signs for rummage sales, garage sales, and House For Sale. Use flashy colors of posterboard and paints. Combine different colors for different kinds of signs. Purple and turquoise for rummage sale signs would be neat. How about blue on orange for garage sale signs? House-for-sale signs could be done in yellow and red.

CUT the signs in the shape that can show the kind of sale being held. People sell lots of things including puppies, kittens, cars, and bicycles.

DRAW the outline of each kind of sign you need on a piece of posterboard. Cut out the sign following the drawing. Use this first one as a pattern for the rest of the signs. Lay it on posterboard and trace around it. The signs should be about two feet wide by two feet high. They could be a little larger or a little smaller.

COAT the signs with hair spray after the paint has dried. This will help preserve the signs.

TAPE a clear plastic pocket along the bottom of the sign. The seller can put a note in the pocket telling the dates and times of his sale. He might want his phone number there. Or a picture of his least favorite relative. It is his decision.

ATTACH some signs to stakes to be pushed into the ground. Other signs could be two-faced. Tape them at the top to make an A-shape. Tape a crosspiece at the bottom. A brick or rock sitting on the crosspiece will keep the sign from blowing away. Don't use your baby brother to hold it in place.

READ the sale ads in the classified section of your newspaper. Find out who is selling what in your neighborhood.

CALL the telephone numbers listed in the ads or visit the addresses. Offer the sellers one of your signs to use on the days of their sales.

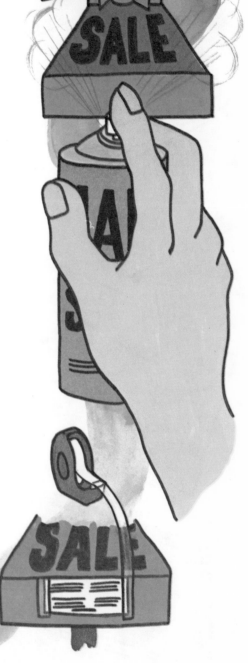

25

KEEP a notebook that shows where you placed signs. Also note when you can pick them up.

GO get your signs right after the sale ends. Offer them for use again and again.

MAKE a portfolio for toting signs. Get two large pieces of posterboard. Find a piece of strong cloth. Cut it 4 inches wide and as long as the longest side of the posterboard. Staple the long side of the cloth to the back of one of the boards along one long side. Staple the other long side of the cloth to the other piece of board in the same way.

JOIN the sides of the boards with four strips of elastic on each side. Cut all the pieces of elastic about four inches long. Staple the strips to the boards to connect them.

CUT OUT four pieces of posterboard. Make them about 6 inches wide and 4 inches high. Center two of the pieces on the inside and outside of one side of the portfolio along the top. Glue them in place. Do the same with the other two pieces on the other side. Ask mother or dad to cut out hand holes in these thick layers of posterboard.

Use Head! Save Feet!

MAKE a list in your mind. Think of places you need to go and things to do. Write a very long list on paper.

SAVE short lists. When the list is longer, do everything together in one day.

FIND friends who are going to the same places. Walk together just for fun. Or share a ride.

ARRANGE your trips in a circle. Go farther and farther away. Then work your way home again.

Every Little Bit

HELP your family put away the next load of groceries. Take off the extra plastic wraps and boxes. Put all these in a heap. Take a good, long look at the size of this heap. Think of ways to bring home fewer wrappings.

LOOK for products that have good packaging. Decide if an outside box is really necessary.

FIND packages that can be easily disposed of. Paper will decompose. Plastic will not. Spray cans are hard to get rid of.

BUY the biggest packages you can. One large cereal box is better than several small ones.

LOOK for returnable bottles.

MAKE less garbage. Flatten cartons and cans. Find containers that can be used over and over.

ORGANIZE your friends or club. Help the whole community to make less garbage.

New Neighbors

IMPORTANT PHONE NUMBERS

Police: 764-1817	School: 662-5740
Fire: 994-3100	Office: 651-9316
Doctor: 663-6621	Babysitter: 7631502
Dentist: 663-8402	Dept. Store: 6624171
Drug Store: 761-7122	Market: 769-8264

FIND information for new neighbors. Make a list of schools, churches, and clubs. Select good stores in the community. Ask adults to recommend doctors and dentists.

MAKE an information card. Index cards work well. On one side write emergency phone numbers. Draw a map on the other side. Put schools, churches, and stores on the map. Include other information that is important in your community.

MAKE lots of copies of the card. Ask your friends to help. Decorate the cards.

FIND new people in town. Check with your school and church. Ask community groups to give you the names of new people.

VISIT the new people. Give them the information card. Stay a few minutes to answer questions.

Partner for a Day

PARTNERS		
NAME		
John Smith •		
Mary Brown • English •		
Nate Turner • Spelling •	6	

NEW STUDENTS		
NO.	NAME	GR.
1.	Joe Elliott	5
2.	Eve Sikes	6
3.	George Ike	2
4.	May East	3
5.	Greg Solak	

SELECT a club or group of friends to work on the project. A student government group is great.

WRITE down the names of all the people who want to be partners for a day. Ask each person to fill in his grade or classes. Add names of clubs and other activities.

MEET with your school principal. Show him your plans. Ask for the names of new students.

FIND OUT about the new student's grade or classes. Ask what kinds of things he likes to do.

MATCH the new student with a good partner.

SHOW your partner around. Answer questions. Introduce him.

Practical Prices

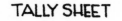

TALLY SHEET

Milk   ⳽⳽⳽⳽ ⳽⳽⳽⳽ |
Eggs   ⳽⳽⳽⳽ ⳽⳽⳽⳽ |
Bread ⳽⳽⳽⳽ |
Hamburger ⳽⳽⳽⳽ ⳽⳽⳽⳽ ||
Flour ||||
Sugar ⳽⳽⳽⳽
Dog Food ||
Chicken   ⳽⳽⳽⳽ ||
Lettuce   ⳽⳽⳽⳽ ⳽⳽⳽⳽
Cabbage ||
Wax Paper |||

FIND friends to work on the pricing project. Ask each friend to collect several grocery lists. Get one at home. Ask your neighbors for lists.

COPY one list on a large piece of paper. Pick up another list. Make tally marks for items already on the master list. Add new items to the list. Some people can tally while others read.

TAKE a good look at the master list. Put check marks by the most common items. Include thirty to sixty items.

ARRANGE the list by sections. Put all the meats together. Make sections for dairy products, fresh produce, and canned food. Make more sections if you need them.

ARRANGE each section in alphabetical order.

LEAVE ROOM for two or three brands and sizes.

TAKE the list to one supermarket. Find each item in the store. Decide what sizes and brands to put on the list. Leave one line for the house brand. It will have a different name in each supermarket.

MAKE a list of the supermarkets in your community. Decide which ones to include. Stores in biking distance are great. Find an adult to drive you to others.

MAKE several good copies of your master list. Fill in the names of the supermarkets.

DIVIDE your friends into teams. Send each team to a supermarket. Walk up and down the aisles with the master list. Write down each price. Put the date at the top of the list.

MEET with all the shopping teams. Combine the prices on one paper.

FIND a way to make lots of copies of the list. An adult may do it at his business. A teacher may be able to help. Be prepared to supply the paper.

DISTRIBUTE the list to shoppers. Give it to everyone who gave you a grocery list. Take it to all your neighbors and friends at school. Pass it around at clubs and meetings.

MASTER LIST

	HUB	C&C	VALU	UPTOWN
DAIRY				
Eggs				
Small	.49	.53	.46	.47
med	.59	.63	.56	.57
large	.69	.73	.66	.67
x-large	.79	.83	.76	.77
Cheese (lb)				
Colby	1.09	1.18	.99	1.15
Cheddar	1.15	1.25	1.09	1.20
Milk				
½ gal.	.63	.73	.59	.69
1 gal.	1.25	1.45	1.45	1.46
PRODUCE				
Carrots (lb)	.39	.35	.29	.33
Celery				
Lettuce				

Hardy Hamburger

RAW MEAT   16 oz.

COOKED MEAT   12 oz.

DIVIDE 16 into 12

.75
16⟌12.00

.75 × 100 = 75% meat

100 − 75% = 25% fat

BUY a package of hamburger and take it home.

BORROW a food scale from a friend. Put a bowl on it. Set the weight at zero.

PLACE the hamburger in the bowl. Write the weight on a piece of paper.

BROWN the hamburger in a fry pan. Drain off as much fat as you can.

PUT the hamburger back into the bowl. Weigh it again. Write the weight down.

DIVIDE the weight of the raw meat into the weight of the cooked meat. The answer is the percentage of meat. Subtract that from 100. The final answer is the percentage of fat.

USE the cooked hamburger to surprise your family with a spaghetti dinner.

BUY hamburger from other stores. Find out the percentage of fat. Add the information to your supermarket price list. Share the work with friends.

Little Letters

STAND UP and be counted. Let people know how you feel about things. Write about things you like. Write about things you don't like. Both kinds of letters are important. They help executives make decisions.

BE SURE you send your letters to the right person. If you like a show on TV, write to the producer. If you don't like a show, write to the sponsor.

WRITE to the editor of your newspaper. He likes to hear what young people think about what is happening in their community. Maybe your letter will be published. Perhaps it will help change things.

SEND letters to your representative and your senators. You can even write to the President.

KEEP your letters short. Write about only one topic.

SIGN the letter. That's very important. If you believe in things, you must be proud to sign your name. Be sure to put your return address on also. Maybe they'll answer you.

Wildlife Today
American Television Network
Dear Mr. Producer.
I watched your show about
saving leaders. It was on
much good job.
TV
you
about
you

To the Editor
The Times

Dear Sir:
I am nine. I hope you care what I say. I think there should be places where I can ride my bike. I think there should be special places. My friend, Herbie, just got hit by a car. He was riding in the street. It's the only place we can ride. If we had special places, he would not be in the hospital.
Yours truly,
Wendy Ball

Everybody's Carrot

MEET with your friends who want a vegetable garden. Plan the details together.

FIND a garden plot. Everyone must be able to get to it easily. It must be large enough to grow vegetables for everyone. Look for a place that has good soil, plenty of sunshine, and a water supply. Ask permission of the owner before you begin.

DECIDE what tools you will need. The library has books about gardening. Collect the tools from the members of your group. Ask permission before you borrow them. Work out a way to put the owner's name on each tool. Paint or heavy tape will work.

TAKE CARE of the tools. Find a dry place to keep them. A garage or shed near the garden is great. Or find a wooden box. Tie loops of clothesline around it for handles. Use the box to carry tools to the garden.

CHOOSE the seeds for the garden. Let everyone choose a favorite vegetable. Decide how many packages of seeds to buy. It will depend on the size of the garden. Check the chart in the back of the seed packages.

DRAW a map of the garden. Make lines for the vegetable rows. Put tall vegetables near a fence or wall. Put plants that insects don't like around the outside.

FIND OUT when each vegetable should be planted. Read library books or check the seed packages. Give some plants an early start indoors.

PLAN a garden planting holiday. Ask everyone to come. Bring garden tools, seeds, and little plants. Remember the map. Work together to plant the garden. Dig the soil, plant the seeds, and label the rows. A garden book will tell you just how to do it. When the work is done, enjoy a picnic and games.

37

SHARE the work in the garden. Make a chart with everyone's name. Keep it with the tools. Each day you work, write the number of minutes on the chart. Trade working time when someone is on vacation.

LOCATE a good water supply. A hose is great, or you may carry buckets of water. Make sure someone waters the garden in dry weather.

PULL weeds regularly. Leave a few at the edge. They will make a good dinner for the insects.

PROTECT the vegetables from the heat. Shade the soil with dead weeds, dry grass, or straw.

LEARN to live with insects. Some are good for the garden. Others must be chased away.

FIND a good gardening book for more information.

38

SHARE the harvest. Figure out how to divide the vegetables. Give everyone the same amount. Or, give more to people who work more. Trade vegetables you don't like for your favorites. Give lots to the owner of the land.

LEARN HOW to pick vegetables. Some plants will keep growing if they're picked carefully.

SAVE some for the winter. Find a book that tells how to dry, freeze, or can the vegetables. Freezing is easy and uses plastic bags. Canning is difficult and uses clean jars. Ask an adult to help with canning. Plan another holiday with your friends. Put up lots of vegetables for the winter.

CLEAN UP the garden patch. Return all the tools to the owners. Throw paper and string in the trash. Leave pulled weeds and old vegetables. They will make the soil better next year.

Shiny Stream, Furry Forest

COLLECT a group of friends to work. Find a stream or pond to take care of. Think small. Select a small stream or part of a larger one. When this project is done, try a larger one.

LOCATE the owners of the land along the stream. Find people who live near the stream. They can direct you to the other owners. Ask permission to take care of the stream.

HIKE along the stream. Take pictures before you start to work.

ORGANIZE a cleaning party. Take large containers. Collect the trash along the stream. Take more pictures after the clean-up. Find a good place to dispose of the garbage.

VISIT adult organizations in your community. Show them the pictures of the stream before and after the clean-up. Ask for help and advice.

FIND specialists to give advice. Science teachers, conservation clubs, and government agencies can help.

LEARN what plants grow well by the stream. Find out the right way to plant them. Their roots will hold dirt out of the water. Go back to the clubs you visited. Ask them to help provide plants. If they cannot, start your own money making projects. Hold a planting party by the stream.

LEARN what animals live by the stream. Find ways to encourage them. Bird houses are a good start.

TRACK DOWN the sources of waste in the stream. An adult who understands science can help.

WRITE polite letters to the businesses that dump waste. Explain what you are doing for the stream. Ask them to help. Write letters to the newspaper.

INVOLVE your community in the work. Continue to visit clubs. Show your pictures to them. Ask the newspaper to send a reporter to the stream with you.

FIND similar projects. A furry forest is a good one. Ask the state forest service to help make a forest on a little piece of barren land.

Rules & Rubies

THINK about your favorite game. Imagine what it would be like if there were no rules. You would not know how to play it. You could not tell anyone else how to play the game. You would not know who won or who lost. Game rules are very important.

THINK about groups you've joined. The first thing you did was learn the rules. You may have started a club. The chances are the first thing you did was make up some rules. Good rules help make a good club. Rules for groups are very important.

THINK about meetings you've gone to. Some were fun. Some were not. Some got a lot done. Some lasted longer than they had to. The good meetings were run by a good set of rules. Meeting rules are very important.

MAKE UP a set of rules for your group meetings. Good rules always reflect the purpose of the group.

DECIDE who is going to be in charge of your meetings. Sometimes that person can't be there. Make up a rule about who takes that person's place.

DECIDE when you will have your regular meetings. Sometimes you have to hold emergency meetings. Make up a rule on how you call emergency meetings.

DECIDE what reports members have to give at meetings. Your group should have a secretary. The secretary takes notes of all that happens at each meeting. These are called the Minutes of the Meeting. The secretary should always read the minutes of the last meeting. This helps members to remember what happened. It also helps members who were absent last time. Your group should have a treasurer, also. Your treasurer should report at each meeting how rich the group is.

DECIDE what other reports should be given at meetings. Special activities should be reported. Set aside special times during the meetings for these reports.

MAKE UP an agenda for your meetings. An agenda is an outline of the meeting. It lists the things to talk about in the meeting. Stick to the agenda. Don't wander off into other things.

DECIDE on the amount of time to spend on each thing on your agenda. Make a rule for stopping discussion. You can spend a whole meeting on just one thing if you're not careful. There are usually a lot of things to talk about.

LOOK AT this word: parliamentarian. It's a big word. It describes a big job. The parliamentarian is a special person in your group. He is the keeper of the rules. He settles arguments about the rules. Decide who is the parliamentarian. The person you pick must be at every meeting.

MAKE UP a rule about what to do when someone breaks the rules.

REMEMBER these rules about rules:

    Good rules are fair to everyone.
    Good rules make things orderly.
    Good rules make things easier.
    Good rules are easy to understand.
    Good rules are easy to follow.
    Good rules make better organizations.

Rules are like rubies. Good ones are very valuable. Bad ones aren't worth anything. A good ruby that no one wants isn't worth anything. A good rule that isn't followed isn't worth anything. Your group will be more fun and more interesting with a good set of rules. It will stay fun and interesting if you follow your rules.

INDEX

ILLUSTRATIONS